The Manatee vs.
the Local Economy

The Manatee vs. the Local Economy

The Cape Coral, Florida, Experience

An Integrated Case Study

Donald A. Forrer, Linda Jackson, Justin McBride,
Elaine Reed Kruse, Rhett Goby, Sue Goby,
Jeff Cull, and Marilyn K. Benson
International College, Naples, Florida

iUniverse, Inc.
New York   Lincoln   Shanghai

The Manatee vs. the Local Economy
The Cape Coral, Florida, Experience

Copyright © 2005 by Donald A. Forrer

iUniverse books may be ordered through booksellers or by contacting:

iUniverse
2021 Pine Lake Road, Suite 100
Lincoln, NE 68512
www.iuniverse.com
1-800-Authors (1-800-288-4677)

ISBN: 0-595-33784-8

Printed in the United States of America

CONTENTS

CASE STUDY AUTHORS

Left to Right–*Marilyn K. Benson*, M.S.M., Assistant to the Dean, School of Business–International College; *Justin McBride*, M.E.M., Senior Environmental Specialist, Division of Natural Resources-Marine Program, Lee County Florida; *Linda Jackson*, M.B.A., Contracts Specialist, Collier County Government; *Donald A. Forrer*, D.B.A., MBA/MPA Program Director/Faculty, International College; *Elaine Reed Kruse*, M.P.A., Business Consultant, Naples, Florida; *Rhett Goby*, M.B.A., Senior Analyst, Fischer International Systems; *Sue Goby*, M.B.A., Business Solutions of Naples, Inc., Naples, Florida, Adjunct Faculty, International College; *Jeff Cull* (not pictured), Reporter, Ft. Myers News-Press.

Special Thanks to:
Rotary Club of Cape Coral for sponsorship of the civic event and to
Ms. Suzanne Ponicsan, Dr. Katherine Dew, Susan Denham, and Cheryl Collins for
their editing assistance, which was appreciated by everyone involved in this project.

ABSTRACT

Faculty and recent graduate students at International College in Naples, Florida completed this economic, environmental, and ethics case study from May 2003 to July 2004. The rights of the Florida Manatee and West Indian Manatee clash with the rights of waterfront homeowners, dock builders, realtors, and multiple federal and state government agencies in Southwest Florida. This study presents and analyzes the issue from the differing sides. Key players include: Save the Manatee Club, Cape Coral Construction Industry Association, Florida Department of Environmental Protection, Florida Marine Contractors Association, Florida Marine Industry, U.S. Army Corps of Engineers, U.S. Fish and Wildlife Service, and the Florida Fish and Wildlife Conservation Commission. Pending changes and future legal action will most certainly cause reaction from the affected parties.

INTRODUCTION

In an effort to study a volatile emotional issue inherent to Southwest Florida that crossed all fields of study in the School of Business, the Graduate Programs of International College decided to research an issue involving Save the Manatee Club and their efforts to reduce manatee deaths. This controversial topic encompassed all of Florida but affected Southwest Florida tremendously. The original participants in the study included five classes from three graduate programs: Master of Business Administration (MBA), Master of Public Administration (MPA), and Master of Environmental Management (MEM). The case authors decided to continue the classroom research and pursue publication. Due to the controversial nature of the issue and its effect on one community in particular, the authors decided to concentrate the case research on the City of Cape Coral and the local dock building industry.

This interdisciplinary issue is interesting, far reaching, and ongoing. A January 2000 lawsuit was filed against the United States Fish and Wildlife Service (USFWS) and the United States Army Corps of Engineers (USACE) by a coalition of environmental organizations; this initiated the process. The basis of the lawsuit brought by environmental groups was that the federal government, i.e. USFWS, was not living up to its mandate to protect the endangered Florida Manatee (*Trichechus manatus latirostris*) as dictated by the Endangered Species Act (ESA). As a result of a January 2001 settlement of the legal action, USFWS declared parts of Lee County, Florida, as *areas of inadequate protection* and stopped issuing permits for single-family dock building in the designated areas.

Local reaction was immediate as dock builders banded together to protest by contending that they had been put out of business. They alleged that the livelihood of many families had been affected. In support, leaders of the real estate industry and many local government officials rallied and concurred.

Due to the publicity and interest, International College graduate classes (under the leadership of Dr. Don Forrer, Dr. Telemate Jackreece, and Dr. Kris Thoemke) used the summer term in 2003 to research the issue with a goal of determining if the following claims could be substantiated:

- The dock building industry was hurt economically
- Real estate values decreased
- Real estate sales were affected

Initial research culminated in a presentation to the public with an open discussion in the City of Cape Coral, Florida, on August 12, 2003. As a result of this open forum and community interest, the authors of this case decided to continue research and seek additional pertinent data and information to augment this case study. This research analyzes the issue from several viewpoints and provides future researchers with as much information as possible. The researched viewpoints include:

- Business
- Regulatory
- Public Administration
- Environmental
- Public Reaction

The central figure in this case is the manatee. The Florida Manatees, also known as sea cows, live in the inland waterways of Florida. Their presence often conflicts with pleasure-seeking and commercial boaters who regularly traverse the areas. As mentioned earlier, this case study analysis attempts to cover this issue from all affected points of view. There are no winners in this situation as it has divided the Southwest Florida community and created animosity (as pictured in Figure 7) for the once loved manatee. It will be years before the wounds of this action are healed and, depending on the final outcome, satisfaction of any of the affected parties is still very much in doubt.

Figure 1. Manatees in their environment.

From Z. Forrer, 2003, photo taken at Everglades City, Florida. Reprinted with permission.

BACKGROUND

Timeline

This timeline is intended to provide an overview of the case. Issues identified in the timeline are discussed in detail later in the analysis.

- January 2000: A coalition of environmental organizations file two lawsuits; one against USFWS and USACE, and another against the State of Florida.

- January 2000: USFWS begins to operate under its mandated draft interim guidance document for ESA Section 7 consultations as they relate to boat dock permitting in the State of Florida. This document allows boat docks to be built as long as a voluntary donation of $546.00 is made to increase marine law enforcement in the affected area. This is known locally as the *Manatee Dock Fee*. If local agencies do not have proper accounts established to receive this fee, the applicant may send the money directly to the National Fish and Wildlife Foundation for future funding to the local area. This fee was considered extortion by many.

- January 2001: The environmental groups and federal officials reach a settlement to provide new protections for manatees. The settlement agreement outlines certain tasks that federal agencies are required to complete in protection of the manatee.

- January 2001: In response to the settlement agreement, USACE revises its *Manatee Key*, which is a map overlay that defines areas of protection for USFWS. This Key is used to perform a preliminary evaluation of boat dock permit applications as they are received. The USACE uses this evaluation to determine if a permit for a proposed project should be sent to the USFWS for consultation.

- February 2001: USFWS designates three parts of Lee County as areas of inadequate protection in reaction to the tasks set forth in the settlement agreement. Based upon this designation, USFWS stopped providing comments on boat dock permits to the USACE, effectively halting the issuance of boat dock permits in all areas designated as areas of inadequate protection.

- May 2001: Florida Governor Jeb Bush sends a letter to the USFWS, requesting that the interim guidance voluntary donation/dock fee be removed. In exchange for a removal of the fee, Governor Bush promises to add monies and additional enforcement to offset the potential loss in revenue to law enforcement.

- July 2002: USFWS argues before a federal judge that the settlement agreement it entered into with the plaintiffs was illegal and should be nullified.

- August 2002: In response to USFWS's argument that the settlement agreement was illegal, a federal judge threatens to find USFWS and its director, Ms. Gail Norton, in contempt of court by citing that they had violated the terms of the settlement agreement. The court had ordered USFWS to finalize its refuges and sanctuaries for the Florida Manatee by November 2002.

- November 6, 2002: USFWS issues its proposed incidental *take* (a term that makes reference to the disturbing of manatee by a watercraft) regulations under the Marine Mammal Protection Act for Florida (MMPA).

- November 2002: Judgment is received stemming from nine Lee County boaters who contested tickets they received from the Florida Fish and Wildlife Conservation Commission (FWC) in 2000. The boaters' argument claimed that the creation of the speed zones (to reduce manatee mortality by watercraft) was against the Florida Constitution and that they were overreaching and overbroad because they were not based on sound science. On November 12, 2002, Circuit Court Judge Jack Schoonover rules in favor of the boaters. This ruling is commonly referred to as *The Schoonover Ruling*. As a result, the speed zones were nullified.

- November 23, 2002: More than 1,000 protesters rally in the City of Cape Coral, Lee County, Florida, to show their opposition to the proposed MMPA rules put forth by USFWS.

- December 2, 2002: More than 2,500 people attend a public hearing in Fort Myers, Lee County, Florida, with USFWS officials to comment on the MMPA proposed rules. The majority of the comments were negative towards the proposed rule.

- January 2003: USFWS and the plaintiffs come forward with a stipulated agreement to the original settlement, which creates new methods for evaluating single-family boat dock permits as well as creates several new refuges and sanctuaries in Southwest Florida. These refuges include new speed zones in the Caloosahatchee River.

- March 3, 2003: Florida Marine Contractors Association, Inc. files a Notice of Intent to sue the Department of the Interior, specifically USFWS. Intent is based on claims of violation of the ESA and for unauthorized assertion of jurisdiction under the MMPA.

- March 2003: Parties involved in the manatee lawsuit meet in Orlando, Florida, to discuss entering conflict resolution. Groups consider delaying manatee protection rules in exchange for not pursuing the down-listing of the state designation of the manatee from endangered to threatened in Florida. This initial effort is unsuccessful.

- May 2003: The FWC files a notice to appeal The Schoonover Ruling, creating a stay of judgment, which allows the speed zones in question to remain enforceable.

- May 2003: USFWS reaches a *no finding* in its *Incidental Take* rulemaking under the MMPA, creating no rule. In the absence of an Incidental Take rule, USFWS must comment on dock permits on a case-by-case basis.

- May 2003: USFWS Director, Steve Williams, releases a memo rescinding the January 22, 2003, management directive on permit consultations.

- May 2003: In a letter addressed to the Lee County manager, Don Stilwell, the U.S. Department of the Interior announces the removal of the area of inadequate protection designation for the Caloosahatchee River, which includes Cape Coral.

- May 2003: A public hearing on the manatee refuges and sanctuaries proposed for the Caloosahatchee River and San Carlos Bay by the USFWS as part of the stipulated agreement with the plaintiffs draws over 3,000 people. The vast majority of the comments are not in favor of the zones as proposed.

- July 2003: The original plaintiffs file a Notice of Controversy in federal court, claiming that USACE and USFWS have once again violated court agreements.

- August 2003: USFWS publishes its final rule for additional manatee refuges and sanctuaries in Lee, Duval, Clay, St. Johns, and Volusia counties (see Figure 2).

Figure 2. County map of Florida.

From the U.S. Census Bureau website. (n.d.) Retrieved May 5, 2004, http://quickfacts.census.gov/qfd/maps/florida_map.html

- August 2003: The City of Cape Coral files a lawsuit in federal court claiming the USFWS has failed to meet statutory timelines under Section 7 of the ESA and that the newly created manatee refuges speed zones are in conflict with the Regulatory Flexibility Act.
- September 2003: USFWS releases *Biological Opinions for Reaches 30, 32, 33* in Lee County. (USFWS uses the term *reach* to define zones of protection.) The Biological Opinion for Reach 30 (10 Mile Canal/Mullock Creek) finds that

the proposed single-family docks are not likely to adversely affect the manatee or its habitat. The Biological Opinion for Reach 32 (Cape Coral) finds that the proposed single-family docks are not likely to adversely affect the manatee or its habitat. The Biological Opinion for Reach 33 (Bokeelia/Pine Island Sound Area) finds that the proposed single-family docks are reasonably certain to affect the manatee in the form of watercraft mortalities (unauthorized incidental take). The Opinion regarding Reach 32 allows the USACE to issue permits for nearly 600 new boat docks.

- September 2003: USFWS begins posting the newly created speed zones in the Caloosahatchee River. Completion of posting the zones and full enforcement are expected to occur in early November 2003.
- November 2003: USFWS amends its Biological Opinion for Reach 33, allowing for docks to be constructed in the area of Pine Island Sound between Cayo Costa Island south of Pelican Bay and Pine Island, south of Bocilla Island.
- December 2003: After granting extension requests on July 17, September 5, and October 1, the appellate court dismisses the FWC's appeal of The Schoonover Ruling, citing that they failed to comply with the appellate rules and the court's prior orders. This dismissal eliminates state and local enforcement of five state-speed zones in Lee County.
- January 2004: In response to The Schoonover Ruling, USFWS stops issuing single-family boat dock permits in USACE Reaches 30 and 31, plus portions of Reaches 32 and 33.
- January 2004: FWC files a legal request asking the Second District Court of Appeal to review the Circuit Court decision (The Schoonover Ruling) and asks the court to reinstate the affected zones while the case is pending. The court agrees to hear the case but does not reinstate the zones.
- February 2004: Lee County Board of County Commissioners begins a process to create local speed zones to compensate for the removal of the five state-speed zones in The Schoonover Ruling.
- February 2004: USFWS issues a press release stating that it is imposing emergency manatee speed zones in light of The Schoonover Ruling. The emergency speed zones are valid for 120 days; during this time the USFWS must publicly declare if they intend to propose permanent zones in the emergency areas. USFWS does announce that it will move forward with the creation of permanent speed zones. Creation of the emergency speed zones and attached enforcement allows boat dock permits to be issued again.
- March 2004: Second District Court of Appeal denies the review of FWC's appeal to overturn The Schoonover Ruling affecting five state manatee speed zones in Lee County.

- March 2004: Lee County announces it will work toward the creation of a county ordinance to create speed zones, which will protect manatees in the areas where the state speed zones were overturned.
- April 2004: Lee County announces formation of the Local Rule Review Committee in response to FWC's announcement that FWC plans to review speed zones in Lee County. The committee is comprised of two representatives appointed by each county commissioner, one boater, and one environmentalist. The committee must report to FWC by August 2004.
- June 2004: Governor Jeb Bush signs Senate Bill 540 requiring FWC to contract for a study of the manatee population near warm water discharge points such as power plants.

Laws Involved

To better understand the scope of events within this case study, the reader should be aware of the influence of relevant laws. The following section outlines the array of laws and regulations that the federal government has at its disposal for manatee and watercraft access regulation in Florida. As noted earlier, the two federal agencies involved as primary players are the USFWS and USACE. Additional laws include:

- Rivers and Harbors Act (1899)
- Marine Protection, Research and Sanctuaries Act (1972)
- Clean Water Act (1972)
- Federal Coastal Management Act (1972)
- Fish and Wildlife Coordination Act (1934)
- National Environmental Policy Act (1969)
- Coastal Zone Management Act (1972)
- Wild and Scenic Rivers Act (1968)
- Endangered Species Act (1973)
- Marine Mammal Protection Act (1972)
- Magnuson-Stevens Act (1996)

All of the laws listed have bearing on the dock permitting process. However, the Marine Mammal Protection Act and the Endangered Species Act exert the most influence.

Marine Mammal Protection Act of 1972 (MMPA)

While the ESA authorizes the take of listed species, the MMPA specifically contains a moratorium on the taking of marine mammals with certain exceptions. The MMPA seeks to authorize allowable amounts of take that will have negligible impact to marine mammal species through development of incidental take regulations.

> "Take" as defined by the MMPA section 3(13), means "to harass, hunt, capture, or kill, or attempt to harass, capture or kill any marine mammal." The act further defines "harassment" as any pursuit, torment, or annoyance which—1) has the potential to injure a marine mammal; or 2) has the potential to disturb a marine mammal. Incidental Take is unintentional or accidental take which might occur during an otherwise lawful activity. ("Service Looking to Develop", 2001).

Passage of the MMPA rule would theoretically allow USFWS to provide some control over the number of manatees that might be killed due to boater/manatee interaction. With no MMPA rule passed for Florida, USFWS utilizes the ESA to protect the West Indian Manatee (*Trichechus manatus*).

The Endangered Species Act of 1973 (ESA)

The ESA allows the take of endangered species. The way in which take is defined differs from that of the MMPA. According to the ESA (n.d.), take is defined as actions that, "…harass, harm, pursue, hunt, shoot, wound, kill, trap, capture, or collect, or attempt to engage in any such conduct." While the ESA provides similar protections under its definition of take, there are other requirements placed upon the USFWS by ESA that cause controversy. In accordance with the ESA, when USFWS lists a species as either threatened or endangered, there are several things that USFWS must do to protect the listed species. These include designation of critical habitat, recovery planning, consultation, and issuing of incidental take permits. Section 7 of the ESA outlines several types of consultation including informal, formal, early, and emergency. The act states that if any federal agency believes that its proposed action (i.e. approval of a permit), may effect a listed species or its critical habitat, the agency must consult, either formally or informally, with the USFWS. If there is a question about the potential for a proposed action to effect either a species or its habitat, most federal agencies initiate consultation to be safe.

With regard to protection of marine wildlife, informal consultation is not required under the ESA. It is purely the initial opening of dialogue between the federal agency and USFWS. It is here where USFWS and the agency determine if a listed species or its critical habitat will be effected.

If the determination is made that the action will not adversely affect either, then formal consultation is not required. In the event that it is determined that the action may adversely effect a listed species or its habitat, then formal consultation proceedings are requested of USFWS by the federal agency. The result of formal consultation is creation of a Biological Opinion of whether or not the proposed project will effect the species or its critical habitat.

When required, USFWS must complete this Opinion within 135 days of initiation of formal consultation by the requesting federal agency. Results of the Biological Opinion are listed as one of three statements: *not likely to adversely affect, not likely to significantly adversely affect,* and *jeopardy-likely to adversely affect.* The latter two results require USFWS to provide *reasonable and prudent* alternatives, and the federal agency can choose its direction in light of these alternatives. USFWS can also choose to issue incidental take permits and allow the project to move forward in its proposed state. However, this is not possible with the Florida Manatee due to the aforementioned fact that incidental take regulations have not been created in Florida. To date, USFWS has created Biological Opinions for Reaches 30, 32, and 33 in Lee County, outlining their recommendations under the consultation guidelines of the ESA.

PERMITTING PROCESS–LEE COUNTY, FLORIDA

The primary federal agency responsible for issuing permits in Lee County for water-access facilities is USACE's Jacksonville District. Federal permits for marine facilities require either an individual permit (single-family dock permit) or a joint environmental resource permit, filed concurrently with the USACE and the Florida Department of Environmental Protection (FDEP). In many instances, USACE will also require a *dredge and fill permit application*, especially for large marina facilities. USACE gains its authority to require permits from the aforementioned Rivers and Harbors Act of 1899 and the Clean Water Act of 1972.

There are six examples of marine facilities operations that may be exempt (in theory) from the federal permit review process. The three listed are nationwide permits:

- NW-3 Maintenance (for previously authorized structure)
- NW-2 Structures in Artificial Canals (for single-family docks)
- NW-28 Modification of Existing Marinas (no expansion, additional dock spaces, slips, or dredging)

USACE's Jacksonville District also issues regional permits in which the proposed project may be exempt from the full permit review process. To qualify for these permits, applicants must follow standard construction precautions, and the project must be determined not likely to adversely affect the manatee. These regional permits are the remaining three exemptions:

- SAJ-20 Private Single-Family Piers in Florida
- SAJ-17 Minor Structures in Florida
- SAJ-33 Private Multi-Family and Government Piers

In the past, USACE also issued State Programmatic General Permits to the FDEP. Through this, USACE has delegated the authority to issue federal permits for certain activities to the state of Florida. Projects that impinge on seagrasses, marshes, or mangroves; affect manatees or their critical habitat; or are located near the Intracoastal Waterway or federal channels do not qualify for the State Programmatic General Permits. These projects must go through the full federal permitting process. It is important to note that the USACE does not regulate protection of the manatee but must work in conjunction with USFWS in order to ensure that the species is protected. Figure 3 shows several refuge areas along the coast in Cape Coral.

9

Figure 3. Federal manatee refuge area.

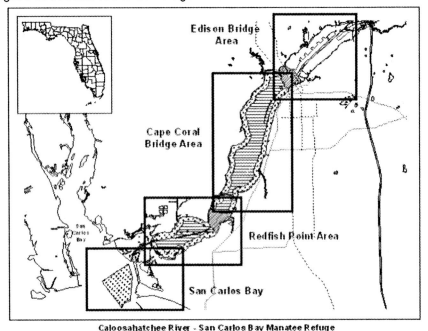

Caloosahatchee River - San Carlos Bay Manatee Refuge

From the United States Fish and Wildlife Service. (n.d.b). Retrieved May 5, 2003, from http://northflorida.fws.gov/Manatee/Maps/lee-overview.htm

Flow Charts of Lee County's Permit Review

All rules, regulations, and proposed regulations previously described, manifest themselves to Florida and Lee County residents most prominently when they apply for water-access permits of various types. With the federal process, it is important to note that the USACE has revoked all local authorities, creating the necessity of a federal permit for all single-family docks. The USACE will not issue a permit without comment of some form from the USFWS. The USFWS has created Biological Opinions for Reaches 30, 32, and 33 in Lee County outlining their recommendations under the consultation guidelines of the ESA.

The federal and state permitting process flow charts outline the potential routes of travel for Lee County permits. The federal (Figure 4) and the state (Figure 5) permitting process occur simultaneously and that neither agency will issue approval until the other has completed their review process. These figures are not comprehensive in nature, but attempt to show the complexities involved with the permitting process.

Figure 4. Federal permitting process outlined.

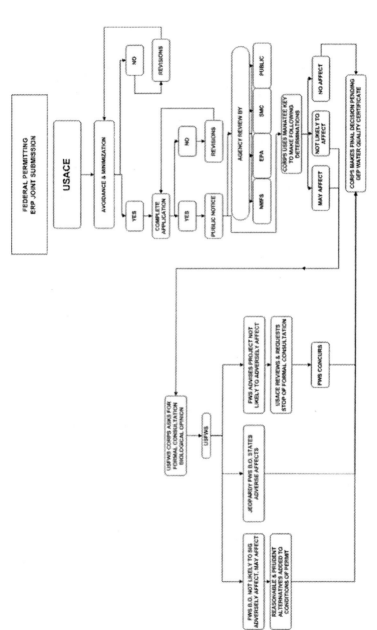

From J. McBride, 2003, Lee County Division of Natural Resources–Marine Program. Reprinted with permission.

Figure 5. State permitting process outlined.

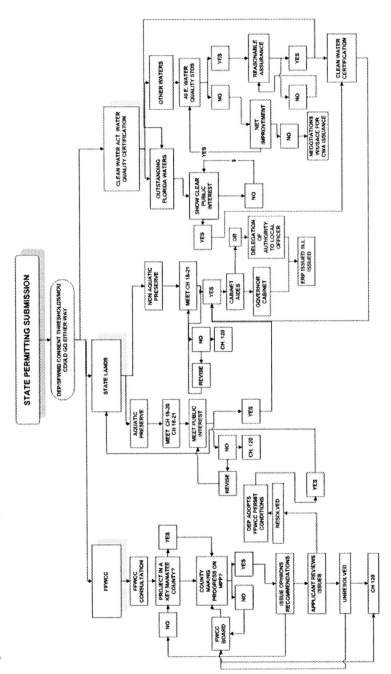

From J. McBride, 2003, Lee County Division of Natural Resources-Marine Program. Reprinted with permission.

KEY PLAYERS IN THIS CONTROVERSY

Save the Manatee Club (SMC)

Formed as a 501(c) 3 organization by former Florida Governor, Bob Graham, and singer/songwriter, Jimmy Buffett, in 1981 to allow public participation in the preservation of the endangered manatee, the SMC has grown to over 40,000 members. The group coordinates public awareness and education projects, manatee research, rescue and rehabilitation efforts, advocacy and legal action through funds from the Adopt-A-Manatee program. One of their goals is to ensure better protection for manatees and their habitat (Save the Manatee, n.d.).

United States Fish and Wildlife Service (USFWS)

The United States Fish and Wildlife Service is a member of the Department of the Interior with offices in every state. As noted throughout this case, USFWS is an active participant in efforts to protect wildlife while still preserving quality of life for United States residents. Their mission is stated on their website.

> *"Working with others to conserve, protect and enhance fish, wildlife, and plants and their habitats for the continuing benefit of the American people describes the organization fairly well"*
> (United States Fish & Wildlife Service, n.d.a).

United States Army Corps of Engineers (USACE)

The United States Army Corps of Engineers (USACE) consists of 40,000 employees working with civilian authorities and business leaders to build our nation's infrastructure. Through a diverse workforce consisting of biologists, engineers, geologists, hydrologists, natural resource managers and other professionals, the USACE works to meet the demand of a growing population throughout the US. The USACE mission, as stated on their web site, describes the organization:

Provide quality, responsive engineering services to the nation including:

- *Providing design and construction management support for other Defense and Federal agencies.*
- *Planning, designing, building and operating water resources and other civil works projects.*
- *Designing and managing the construction of military facilities for the Army and Air Force.*

(United States Army Corps of Engineers, n.d.).

Florida Fish and Wildlife Conservation Commission (FWC)

The Fish and Wildlife Conservation Commission was created by a constitutional amendment approved in the 1998 General Election as part of the package proposed by the Constitutional Revision Commission. The agency is designated to provide consistently increasing or stable wildlife population within the state of Florida. Their mission is listed on their web site.

"Managing fish and wildlife resources for their long-term well being and the benefit of the people"
(About FWC, 2004).

Standing Watch (SW)

The boaters' coalition, Standing Watch, was formed in 2000 to represent boaters' rights in the state of Florida. With over 20,000 members, the organization continues to grow. Their mission, as listed on their web site and stated below, describes the organization.

"To protect our rights to use Florida waterways as responsible stewards of our natural resources" (Standing Watch, n.d.).

To support this mission we will:

- *Organize the boaters of Florida in a proactive, environmentally responsible force*
- *Seek and disseminate relevant information with a combination of the latest scientific methods and hands-on common sense experience*
- *Support and defend out boating rights in any and every necessary arena*
- *Provide information for members on present and pending legislation*
- *Be an advocate of boater education, safety*
- *Be a conduit for communication between Florida's recreational boaters and our policy makers*
- *Highlight positive aspects of our statewide boating community* (Standing Watch, n.d.).

Florida Marine Industry (FMI)

The Florida Marine Industry Association serves its members through education programs and certification classes, seminars, Clean Boating Partnership's Clean Marina and Boatyard programs. The Association also sponsors events and groups such as Monofilament Madness Waterway Clean-up and the Caloosahatchee River Citizen's Association. Their mission, as listed on their web site and stated below, describes the organization:

- *To promote and protect recreational boating as a traditional family pastime*
- *To protect and enhance the environment and Florida's waterways*
- *To promote boating safety for all of Florida's recreational boaters*
- *To preserve every citizen's right to access Florida's waterways*
- *To promote Florida boating and fishing as a tourism attraction and*
- *To represent, educate and advance Florida's marine industry business and workforce* (Florida Marine Industry, n.d.)

Cape Coral Construction Industry Association (CCCIA)

The Cape Coral Construction Industry Association (CCCIA) was established for the benefit of those engaged in construction and construction related industries in the City of Cape Coral. The purpose of the organization continues to be bringing together those that work and benefit from the construction industry, to network, to meet others, share information and speak with one voice on issues that impact the industry on a local, state, and national level (P. Schnell, personal communication, January 5, 2004). Their mission is stated on their website.

- *To present a unified voice in matters relating to the construction industry*
- *To encourage and establish a professional standard of conduct for CCCIA members*
- *To provide educational and professional development through quarterly builder and sub-contractor workshops. CEU (continuing education credits) are offered to satisfy state requirements*
- *To provide an opportunity to interact, share, and communicate with other CCCIA members' and the community* (Cape Coral Construction Industry Association, n.d.)

Florida Marine Contractors Association (FMCA)

The Florida Marine Contractors Association, Inc. (FMCA) was established in 1999 as a non-profit Florida corporation. The organization is dedicated to enhancing the business environment of highly qualified and credentialed general and marine contractor members. In five years, FMCA has established the political clout and the resources to influence events of vital concern to the marine construction industry and to the construction and marine industries at large. Their mission as listed on their web site is extremely detailed and describes the organization's mission and goals. Their motto, "No Greater Credential" is inclusive of those goals (Florida Marine Contractors Association, n.d.).

REACTION TO THE FEDERAL CASE

Initial Response

When a coalition of environmental organizations filed their legal action in January of 2000 against USFWS, USACE, and the State of Florida, the political controversy that would follow could not have been anticipated. USFWS immediately responded with a quick fix known as draft interim guidance. This guidance attempted to provide funds to protect the manatee by allowing boat docks to be built as long as a voluntary donation of $546.00 was made to increase law enforcement in the affected area.

This was quickly labeled as extortion and protested vehemently. In May 2001, Florida Governor Jeb Bush requested that the interim guidance voluntary fee be removed. In exchange for removal of the fee, Governor Bush promised to add additional enforcement to offset the potential loss in revenue to law enforcement.

In January 2001, environmental groups and federal officials agreed on a settlement providing new protections for manatees and outlining tasks that the federal agencies are required to complete to protect the manatee. This caused reaction from USACE as they revised their Manatee Key. The USACE uses the Manatee Key to perform a preliminary evaluation of boat dock permit applications. Additionally, USACE uses the results from this evaluation to determine if a project should be sent to the USFWS for consultation on Manatee issues. If all regulations are met, a permit is issued.

In February 2001, USFWS designated three parts of Lee County as areas of inadequate protection in completion of the tasks set forth in the settlement agreement. Based upon this designation, USFWS stopped providing comments on boat dock permits to USACE, effectively halting the issuance of boat dock permits in all areas designated as areas of inadequate protection. This action caused the public to take notice. The controversy officially became a public issue directly affecting industries in Southwest Florida. Community unrest caused by the stoppage of permits continued as more than 1,000 protesters rallied in Cape Coral to show their opposition to the proposed MMPA rules put forth by the USFWS on November 23, 2002. Additionally, on December 2, 2002, approximately 2,500 people attended a public hearing in Fort Myers with USFWS officials to comment on the MMPA proposed rules. The majority of the comments were negative towards the proposed rule (Cull & Hayford, 2003).

As research indicates, this was just the beginning of action and reaction as the federal government, state government, local government, building industry, public activists, and environmental groups all work for an agreement that will protect their interests. In this case, interests are varied enough that it seems impossible to reach common ground that will satisfy all parties and protect the manatee.

Environmental Issues

In the eyes of some environmental groups, years of inadequate manatee protection led to the current situation. Increasing manatee mortality caused by watercraft collisions (see Figure 6 and Table 1) compelled several environmental groups, led by the Save the Manatee Club, to take legal action. This began a process that will affect Southwest Florida for this decade and beyond.

Figure 6. Manatee watercraft mortalities.

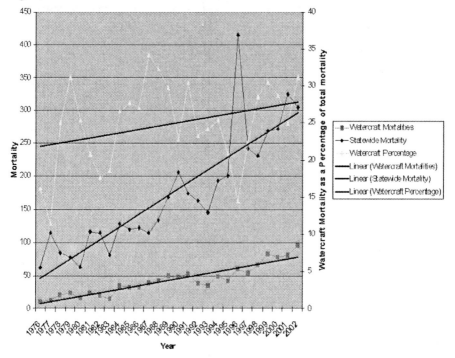

From Florida Fish and Wildlife Conservation Commission Manatee Mortality Database. (n.d.a). Retrieved May 5, 2003, from http://myfwc.com/manatee/data_search.htm

After a long period of legal wrangling, the issue gained attention in May of 2003 when the USFWS concluded no finding in its incidental take rulemaking under the MMPA, creating no rule. In the absence of an incidental take rule, USFWS must comment on dock permits on a case-by-case basis. This effectively delayed dock building in Southwest Florida and created uncertainty in the construction industry (Cull, 2003c).

Table 1. Manatee mortality in Lee County vs. State of Florida.

Place	Water-craft	Canal Lock	Other Human	Perinatal	Cold Stress	Natural	Undet-ermined	Un-recovered	Total
Lee-98	9	0	3	8	1	5	5	0	31
FL-98	66	9	6	53	9	12	72	4	231
Lee-99	10	1	1	6	0	0	6	9	33
FL-99	82	15	8	53	5	37	69	0	269
Lee-00	13	0	1	8	1	11	8	2	44
FL-00	78	8	8	58	14	37	61	8	272
Lee-01	23	0	0	6	5	4	13	0	51
FL-01	81	1	8	62	31	34	106	2	325
Lee-02	13	0	2	9	5	16	13	0	58
FL-02	95	5	9	53	17	59	65	2	305
Lee-03	9	0	0	10	8	45	8	1	81
FL-03	73	3	7	71	47	102	67	10	380

Note. Yearly Mortality Summaries. (n.d.). Florida Marine Research Institute. Retrieved May 5, 2003, from http://research.myfwc.com/manatees/search_summary.asp

The environmental coalition felt that the State of Florida had not done enough to protect the manatee. Therefore, depending on which set of statistics the reader views, manatees were dying at an alarming rate, and boaters were a huge contributor to the problem.

The May 2003 ruling created immediate controversy as the marine industry, construction industry, and local government officials predicted economic problems. According to some economists, Bonita Springs could lose as much as $51 million. Considering that Bonita Springs has far less vacant waterfront property than Cape Coral, based on this estimate, the economic impact in Cape Coral could be far greater. Due to a local 90.6% manatee survival rate versus 94 to 96% for the rest of the state, this proposed rule (actually, the lack of such a rule) allows dock permits throughout Florida, but not in Southwest Florida. Once FWS files with the Federal Register, the rule will go into effect in 30 days and dock building will be curtailed (Cull, 2003c).

Table 2. Manatee aerial survey counts.

	1/22 2003	1/9 2003	3/1 2002	1/6 2001	1/27 2000	1/17 2000	3/6 1999	2/26 1999	1/6 1999
Survey Numbers	3,113	2,861	1,796	3,276	2,223	1,630	2,353	2,034	1,873

Note. Cull, (2003b). Adapted with permission.

SMC also scrutinized efforts by Lee County to implement a state mandated Manatee Protection Plan (MPP). It is the view of SMC that once implementation and enforcement of an accepted plan over the entire county is in place, SMC could support building single-family docks. To satisfy this concern, state and federal authorities reviewed the Lee County initial draft plan and comments were reviewed on May 6, 2003. A subsequent draft was sent to the USFWS and the State of Florida in January of 2004. It is felt that implementation of this plan could provide a comfort level to state and federal authorities that could serve to protect the manatees in Lee County (Duffy, 2003a). USFWS frequently cites the lack of a County MPP in its Biological Opinions for multi-slip and single-family docks in Lee County.

Environmental groups continue to be concerned that the manatee is inadequately protected. It is their position that docks can be built, but protection must be in place. When the federal government lifted the area of inadequate protection designation in Lee County in May 2003, environmentalists were largely quiet. Attorneys for the group indicated that it was premature to determine if the group will go back to court for this ruling. This action effectively freed approximately 600 local dock permits. However, speed zones are still an issue at this time and the federal government's lifting of this designation does not change the requirement for these zones. Environmental groups are currently waiting on future action (Duffy, 2003b).

Table 3. Florida boat registration.

	2001	2002	2003
Florida Boat Registration	902,964	922,597	978,225

Note. Boat Registrations, (2003). Adopted with permission.

Speed zones are another controversial issue. Authorities use speed zones for several reasons including human and wildlife safety. While manatee deaths are thought to be the result of additional boats on the waterways, the human death toll is also a vital statistic when deciding where to enforce speed zones. Statistics released by FWC's Division of Law Enforcement show that human deaths increased from 54 in 2002 to 64 in 2003. The basic issue is that more and more boats are using the waters in and around Florida ("Boat Registrations", 2004). It is widely felt that dock permits and boat ownership are heavily correlated with manatee deaths in Southwest Florida.

Figure 7. Changing perceptions about the manatee.

"Manatee Zones"

From Endangered Outlaw. Reprinted with permission. Retrieved May 5, 2003, from http://endangeredoutlaw.com/designs.htm

STAKEHOLDER REACTION

Public Reaction

The Florida Manatee enjoyed many years of being a favorite among the citizens of Florida. This feeling was extended to SMC when it was formed in 1981. The SMC experienced rapid growth, the state created a license plate to support the manatee preservation, and Floridians searched local waters in hopes of showing visitors from the North this huge creature that makes its home in our local waters. After all, what was there to dislike about the lovable yet elusive manatee? However, if public reaction to recent rulings is an indicator, that perception has changed dramatically in Southwest Florida, especially among boaters.

In the aftermath of the decision to withhold dock building permits and create new state and federal speed zones, reaction from the boating industry, building industry, and especially the dock building industry was negative towards those championing manatee protection. The controversy divided the community and the SMC bore the brunt of public wrath concerning this issue.

A News-Press article on October 24, 2003 quoted a public official as saying, "A lot of people were still eager to protect the manatee, but I think the Save the Manatee Club is losing in the good graces of the public" (Cull, 2003d). He went on to say that public opinion on this topic was changing.

In fact, much has changed since past Governor Bob Graham and Jimmy Buffet formed the SMC to provide public awareness and education about the manatee. Today, the group is not only a steadfast ally of the lovable manatee but is making headlines throughout Florida demonstrating the tenacity in which they work to protect the rights of the manatee. Sadly and more recently, angry letters from citizens force the group's headquarters in Maitland, Florida to keep its doors locked (Cull, 2003c).

Determining the popularity of the manatee would take a detailed study. However, local reaction indicates that rules to protect the manatee made and proposed by federal and state authorities are not popular. As mentioned earlier, the proposed rule changes by USFWS in the MMPA drew more than 1,000 protestors in Cape Coral and Fort Myers, Florida (Cull, 2002). Essentially, anytime there is an opportunity to voice opposition to proposed rule changes, the public is out in force and speaks against any changes in the law.

This issue has clearly become a political football in Southwest Florida. While SMC continues to push for increased regulations as required in the legal settlement, most public figures have placed their allegiance with the building and marine industry. At one end of the spectrum, a marine biologist from the SMC indicates that the Caloosahatchee River is the deadliest river for manatees in Florida. In contrast, the president of Fast Cat Ferry claims the proposed laws will put him out of business due to the added time it will take to get to the mouth of the river. It is important to note that Fast Cats Ferry did go out of business, but an in-depth analysis would be necessary to determine the exact cause (Cull, 2003a).

The suspension of permit issuance by USACE caused many dock builders to make decisions on whether to comply with requirements or continue to build docks without permits mandated beyond local requirements. The City of Cape Coral still issued building permits for docks while placing the responsibility on the homeowner or dock builder to obtain permits from the USACE. This stopped in January of 2003 when USACE filed cease and desist orders against Williamson and Sons Marine Construction followed closely by Honc Marine Contracting in reaction to this policy. This action by USACE elucidated the possible negative economic impact for many employed or supported by this industry. The issue also caused stress in the construction industry as employees feared losing their jobs (Cull, 2003a).

Standing Watch and the Cape Coral Construction Industry Association are among the leaders in the fight to keep federal regulations at a minimum. Additionally, the manatee/dock building issue gained the support of the building industry from local politicians such as Lee County Commissioner Andy Coy and Cape Coral's City Council.

Figure 8. Local photograph of mailbox.

From J. McBride, 2003. Reprinted with permission.

Overall, the majority of public opinion sided with boaters and builders. One common quote from an unknown source was that "this ruling was analogous to determining that stopping the construction of garages would save lives on the highway" (Anonymous personal communication, n.d.). Another popular comment regarded how a boater in Southwest Florida can have six boats in his or her backyard but cannot protect one of them with a dock and lift. Many residents indicate that they are waiting to buy a boat until the issue is resolved (Cull, 2003c). This sentiment appears to be consistent among citizens quoted in the local papers.

Public Administration Reaction

Cape Coral Legal Action

Immediate attention was drawn to the plight of the dock builders in Lee County with special emphasis on the Cape Coral area. On December 13, 2002, Governor Jeb Bush made a statement that the federal government had gone over the line with a dock moratorium in Southwest Florida. Governor Bush noted that a moratorium could devastate the local economy by killing the marine construction industry, slowing boat sales, and lowering coastal property values (Whitehead, 2002).

Throughout this case study, Cape Coral remains steadfast in its defense of the local economy. In late August 2003, the USACE released over 600 pending dock permits. The City of Cape Coral Council voted to proceed in filing a lawsuit against USFWS over the permitting issue and creation of speed zones. Cape Coral City Manager, Terry Stewart, indicated that Cape Coral officials were concerned about future action including speed zones and withholding dock permits that could affect building in Cape Coral (Cull, 2004e).

Cape Coral officials expect to spend between $250,000 and $300,000 to ensure that construction will not be affected in the future. Lee County agreed to pay $50,000 of the legal bills, and (as of June 2004) Cape Coral has expended approximately $387,312 (Cull, 2004e). There are many arguments as to whether this lawsuit is a wise expenditure of taxpayers' money. But to this point, City Council believes that trusting USFWS and the USACE is not a viable option; therefore, the lawsuit went forward in September of 2003.

On September 2, 2003, Cape Coral City Manager, Terry Stewart, sent a letter to Governor Jeb Bush explaining Cape Coral's opposition to the USFWS for failure to process permits within the 150-day time period specified and opposition to future speed zones. Mr. Stewart informed Governor Bush that Cape Coral filed legal action to support Cape Coral's position.

The legal action filed by Cape Coral (Civ. No. 2:03-cv-479-FtM-29SPC) alleges and argues that:

- The statute in the *Clean Water Act* related to proposed construction sites in manatee areas was violated due to USFWS's noncompliance with statutory deadlines
- The designation of the Caloosahatchee River and San Carlos Bay as a manatee protection area should be removed

Figure 9. Local map of Cape Coral canals.

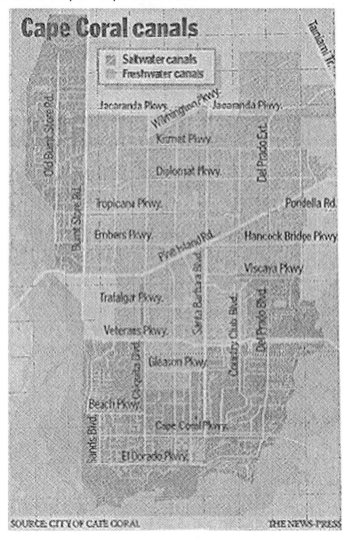

From Cull, (2004c). Adapted with permission.

The City of Cape Coral claims that the economic harm to the citizens of Cape Coral resulted from the two actions and bases its argument on statutes in the ESA, the MMPA, the Clean Water Act, and the Regulatory Flexibility Act. The first three have been cited throughout this case. The Regulatory Flexibility Act, as amended by Title II of Public Law 104-121, and the Small Business Regulatory Enforcement Fairness Act, addresses requirements for consideration of impact on small businesses prior to issuing a federal ruling.

In its legal action, the City of Cape Coral alleges that economic harm has befallen Cape Coral due to the failure of USFWS and USACE's issuance of dock building permits in accordance with the statutory deadlines. USFWS had the following response to a *motion to dismiss*:

- Cape Coral cannot demonstrate that an injury in fact can be shown by Cape Coral

- There is no connection between Cape Coral's allegations and the focus of the complaint, and the challenged action must be caused by the defendant and not a third party

The motion to dismiss concludes that the burden of proof is on Cape Coral to support economic damage caused by actions taken. USFWS contends that Cape Coral's assertion that an unfavorable regulatory environment caused an adverse impact on development, property sales, home sales, business, and property values is not supported. These cannot be directly attributed to any action by the federal agencies involved. Additionally, the motion to dismiss claims that Cape Coral cannot bring suit on behalf of its citizens under the circumstances of this case. Several cases are cited as precedent. At the time of this writing, the motion to dismiss has not been exercised.

Cape Coral's Economic Development Director, Mr. Michael Jackson, responded in a declaration that Cape Coral had been adversely affected due to scores of home purchases and several high value construction projects being cancelled. The realty industry leaders in Cape Coral estimated the negative impact on higher value property and development were between 10% to 35% between the 4th Quarter of 2002 and the 1st Quarter of 2003. Additionally, Mr. Jackson's declaration estimates Cape Coral ad valorem taxes are adversely affected in the areas of property values, impact fees, franchise fees, and other forms of fees levied on the affected property. According to Mr. Jackson's declaration, the City of Cape Coral states:

- Ad valorem taxes fund 53% of Cape Coral's operating budget

- Cape Coral has 400 miles of man-made canals

- Cape Coral's Geographic Information System (GIS) shows 38,469 waterfront properties exist

- 4,776 dock permits are currently recorded, which is only 20% of capacity
- Sales of waterfront homes suffered from price flattening, extended time on market, and even non-sale
- The Cape Coral Real Estate Association reports that during the 4th Quarter of 2002 and 1st Quarter of 2003, scores of buyers cancelled purchases valued from $150,000 to more than $1 million
- Cape Coral's most expensive developments reported that they suffered cancellations and as much as 18 months of inactivity. This is attributed to dock permit interruptions
- Realty industry leaders estimate that uncertainty over dock permitting resulted in a negative impact on this segment of the market ranging from 10% to 35%
- Real estate professionals estimate a $65,000 to $85,000 addition to property value when a dock is built
- The same group estimates an appropriate average waterfront lot is $300,000 and it is reasonable to estimate the average permitted home value at $500,000
- Cape Coral's ad valorem rate is $6.1049/$1,000
- Based on this, Cape Coral's lost revenue for delay of sale or construction of a waterfront home would be $3,052
- Each 100 permits would cost the City $305,200
- Impact fees collected on one single-family home include: $1,115 for parks, $253 for fire, $864 for water, $1,572 for sewer, and $1,379 for roads. This totals $5,183. Additionally, Lee County schools lose $2,232
- Electricity franchise fees are 6% of revenues ($120 per year from each new home)
- Additional fees include: $44 for zoning, $0.10 per square foot (radon), $30 concurrency, and $25 landscaping
- 1,680 or 42% of the businesses in Cape Coral are affected by the real estate industry

The motion to dismiss filed by USFWS contends that these facts have not been proven sufficiently, and there is no casual effect linking actions covered in the lawsuit and any alleged economic hardships experienced by the City of Cape Coral. On September 26, 2003, Governor Bush responded to Mr. Stewart with hope that Cape Coral would consider mediation as opposed to legal action.

Public Administration Reaction–Lee County

While a state-driven issue, the Lee County Manatee Protection Plan (MPP) has bearing upon this case study. It is worthwhile to review relevant points on the plan. The impetus to develop MPP came from two comparable efforts.

The first was generated from the Florida Manatee Recovery Team, an interagency group of manatee experts who developed a Florida MPP. This was approved by the USFWS in 1989 and updated in 1996. One of the tasks identified in the plan was to develop a site specific MPP at the local level. The Florida MPP ranks this task as a priority with regard to the recovery of the manatee.

The second driving factor in the creation of the MPP occurred in October 1989 when the Governor and Cabinet directed 13 key counties to develop an MPP. Included in this plan were the following components:

- An inventory of boat facilities (marinas, docks, boat ramps, dry storage areas, etc.)
- An assessment of boating activity patterns
- Manatee sighting and mortality information
- A boat facility citing plan to determine the best areas for new marinas, boat ramps, etc
- Manatee protection measures, such as boating speed regulations in areas with high boat and manatee usage
- Information on aquatic preserves, outstanding Florida waters, ports, manatee refuges, etc., within Lee County
- An education and awareness program for the public and boaters, divers, and school children
- A water quality and habitat protection program (including land acquisition, and aquatic plant control plans for manatee areas)

The FWC encouraged the county MPP to be adopted as an amendment to the counties' comprehensive plans (Countywide Manatee Protection Act.) This direction from the Florida governor had no legal ramifications and was simply a suggestion.

In 2000, Governor Bush stated that he would not approve any submerged land leases that came before the cabinet and trustees in counties that did not have an approved MPP or were making a *significant progress* according to the Bureau of Protected Species Management. Even with this new directive, there was still no legal requirement for counties to create a MPP.

The majority of the 13 Florida counties complied with the FWC directive and established plans. In a letter dated August 7, 2001 to Mr. David B. Struhs, Department of Environmental Protection, Bradley J. Hartman, Director of the Office of Environmental Services, noted four counties that had not made significant progress. Those counties included Brevard, Lee, Palm Beach and Volusia counties (see Table 4).

Out of the four counties that reported not to have made progress in 2001, only one remains at a draft status, and that was Lee County. Citrus County was the first and only county to adopt an MPP as an element of the comprehensive plan and to go through the five-year review cycle.

In the County Manatee Protection Plan Significant Progress Statement of August 3, 2002, Lee County was identified as a county that did not have a state approved MPP. In 1994, Lee County submitted a draft of their MPP plan; however, it was found to be unacceptable by the Department of Environmental Protection.

Table 4. County progress chart.

County	Separate Marina Citing Study	Boating Activity Study	Manatee Protection Plan	FWC Manatee Protection Rule
Brevard	In MPP	Yes	Approved 2003	Yes
Broward	No	No	Partial Plan 4/92. Comp. Plan amend. 2001	Yes
Citrus	Yes	Yes-for part of county	Approved 1991 Revised 1997	Yes
Collier	Yes	In MPP	Approved 1995	Yes
Dade	No	Yes	Approved 1995	Yes
Duval	No	Yes	Approved 1999	Yes
Indian River	No	Yes	Approved 2000, Amended and approved 2002	Yes
Lee	Yes	Yes	Draft Elements	Yes
Martin	Yes, BOCC app. 2001 and 2002	Yes	Approved 2002	Yes
Palm Beach	Yes	Yes	No	Yes
Sarasota	Yes	Yes	Under FWC Contract	Yes
St. Lucie	Yes	Yes	Approved 2002	Yes
Volusia	Yes-under review by FWC (2002)	Yes	Partial Plan Approved 2001	Yes

Note. The FWC website. Retrieved May 5, 2002, from http://myfwc.com/manatee/rules.htm

In an effort to comply, Lee County has implemented numerous manatee education programs for county residents and visitors. In June 2001, Lee County held a manatee training workshop for local, state, and federal law enforcement. The FWC funded a draft countywide Boat Facility Citing Plan in 1999/2000. Since 1997, Mote Marine Laboratory has conducted four boaters studies in Lee County waters. The latest study concentrated on boater compliance at the mouth of the Caloosahatchee River. However, because Lee County had not continued with the development or implementation of the draft boat facility citing plan, as outlined by the FWC, it was concluded that significant progress was not currently being made.

On February 25, 2003, Lee County commissioners voted unanimously to send a MPP to the state: however, both developers and manatee advocate groups said it was inadequate. The plan would have to be approved by FWC Executive Director, Ken Haddad, and then adopted by Lee County commissioners. There was apprehension among attendees in the meeting about the plan. Basically, there was not enough conclusive evidence on where dock building would and would not be allowed nor was there credible manatee morality statistics and studies. This plan was to be reviewed and commented on and returned to Lee County by the end of April 2003 (Gillis, 2003a).

On March 25, 2003, FWC staff members were advised not to discuss Lee County's controversial MPP. The political atmosphere surrounding the plan was the reason for the gag order (Gillis, 2003c). By USFWS guidelines, the plan must be approved by July 2004.

Based on progressive action by many groups, Florida now recognizes Lee County as making significant progress in their quest to develop a comprehensive MPP plan. Drafts of the Lee County MPP were developed in July of 2003 and January of 2004.

In reality, there are two Florida statutes that outline the content of the MPP. The Florida Department of Community Affairs (DCA) utilizes Florida Statute 380.06.24 (k) to evaluate an MPP. Creation of an MPP, which meets these standards, allows proposed marinas to apply for Development of Regional Impact exemptions. The statute that FWC utilizes to evaluate an MPP, is F.S. 370.12(2)(t)1. It is this statute that was recently amended to include a due date for MPP submissions.

The FWC and the DCA are currently in discussion to create one standard for creation and review of the county MPP at the state level. Even with the newly enacted statutory requirements that place a due date on counties for submission of an MPP, there is no punishment listed for counties that do not approve an MPP by the July 2004 date. Additionally, there is still no formal federal recognition of MPP. The most recent Lee County MPP draft was sent to both the state and federal agencies in February of 2004. The Lee County Board of County Commissioners has received comments from both state agencies and the USFWS. Lee County is currently considering its options in moving forward with adoption of the plan.

In addition to the fact that there was no legal impetus which faced Lee County by not having the MPP in place earlier, there was the fact that the state mandated MPP did not address single-family docks. Therefore, by statute, Lee County does not have to address single-family docks. The State of Florida's threshold of interest ends at groupings comprised of five docks. This point has driven many of the legal actions. To date, in Lee County, there have been no submerged land lease applications denied by the Board of Trustees as a result of Lee County's not having an approved MPP.

Lee County is currently listed by the FWC Bureau of Protected Species Management as a county that is making *significant progress* on their MPP. Yet remaining within Lee County is the issue of the non-release of dock permits by the USACE based upon reports of areas of inadequate protection by the USFWS. It is this issue that has sparked heated discussions between Lee County commissioners, Cape Coral city manager, Lee County citizens, and the dock building industry. It is perceived that this recurring situation is affecting the economic stability of business within Lee County.

To further complicate the issue, there are several identified areas of inadequate protection where the USFWS determined there is a deficiency in one of three areas: speed zones (see Figure 10), signage, and/or enforcement. When an area of inadequate protection is reviewed, the USFWS returns a Biological Opinion, which states that any proposed docks (all docks, including single-family) will negatively affect manatee populations.

Figure 10. Manatee speed zones.

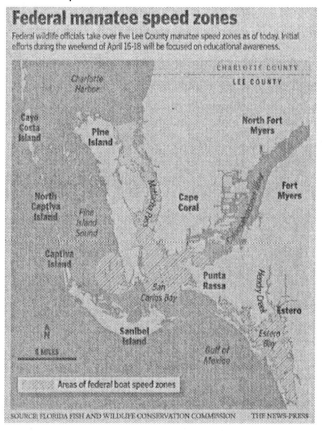

From Cull, (2004d). Adopted with permission.

The USACE will deny any permit applications in these areas. The USFWS feels that either enforcement, signage, or speed zones are needed to remove the areas of inadequate protection. Once again, public administration within Lee County is faced with yet another hurdle in their continued efforts to develop an accepted MPP and to allow single-family boat dock permits to be released.

Manatee Speed Zones: Boaters' Legal Action

In November 2002, a judgment was reached stemming from nine Lee County boaters contesting tickets they received from the FWC in 2000. The boaters' argument claimed that the creation of the speed zones was against the Florida Constitution due to the fact that they were overreaching and overbroad because they were not based on sound science. On November 12, 2002, Circuit Court Judge Jack Schoonover ruled in favor of the boaters. This ruling is commonly referred to as *the Schoonover ruling*. As noted earlier in this case study, this ruling was upheld during the appeal process. Since the time of the appeals, USFWS created emergency speed zones in the five affected areas and is currently in the process of creating permanent speed zones in these areas.

ECONOMIC IMPACT

Lee County Demographics

In order to allow readers to understand this complicated case study, it is important to note some key economic facts about the area. Cape Coral is the largest city in Lee County, Florida; therefore, county statistics play a vital role in any economic impact felt by the city. Over the years, Cape Coral has become known as mainly a retirement city with a population base skewed toward the elderly. However, this is rapidly changing due to the influx of younger workers, mainly in the construction industry. In fact, Lee County is struggling to build schools fast enough to support the younger population moving to the area with children. The City of Cape Coral has 24.6% of the population of Lee County. This figure (see Table 5) includes an 8.1% increase during the past year. This increase is the biggest in the county and nearly twice the average increase for Lee County as a whole.

It is important to note that an 89.2% increase in natural resources, mining, and construction is twice the Florida average and that the 77.2% professional and business services increase kept pace with the State of Florida (see Table 6). Lee County is growing rapidly and, as noted in Table 5, Cape Coral is leading the way.

Table 5. Population by city.

Lee County, Florida Population (2003)

Area	Population	% of Total	% Change 2002 to 2003
Cape Coral	122,373	24.6%	8.1%
Ft. Myers	52,527	10.6%	2.3%
Bonita Springs	39,906	8%	1.9%
Ft. Myers Beach	6,792	1.4%	0.8%
Sanibel	6,224	1.3%	1.5%
Unincorporated	269,200	54.2%	4.2%
Lee Total	497,022	100%	4.6%

Note. Lee County Economic Development Council website. (n.d.b). Retrieved May 5, 2003 from
http://www.leecountybusiness.com/communityoverview/population/population.html

Table 6. Lee County change in employment.

Lee County Florida Change in Employment by Sector (2003)

	Actual Change 1994-2003	Lee % Change	Florida % Change	US % Change
Nat. Resources, Mining & Construction	10,700	89.2%	45.3%	31.9%
Manufacturing	600	10.7%	-13.8%	-14.7%
Retail Trade	7,800	33.1%	16.3%	10.5%
Information	1,200	35.3%	23.2%	42.9%
Financial Activities	2,200	25.3%	25.3%	16.1%
Professional & Business Services	11,500	77.2%	76.6%	36.7%
Education & Health Services	-500	-9.2%	26.6%	41.9%
Leisure & Hospitality	5,000	27.5%	20.0%	30.9%
Other Services	2,600	43.3%	28.8%	21.8%

Note. Lee County Economic Development Council. (n.d.a). Retrieved May 5, 2003 from http://www.leecountybusiness.com

While Lee County is growing, the average income still remains below the Florida and US average. The average wages for the US are $29,264; Lee County $31,817; and the Sate of Florida $36,129 (Lee County, 2003a).

Figure 11. Lee County employment by industry.

Lee County Employment by Industry (2003)

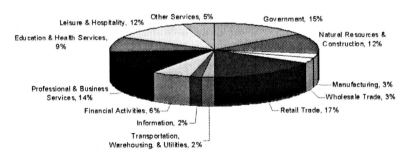

From Lee County Economic Development Council. (n.d.a). Retrieved May 5, 2003, http://www.leecountybusiness.com

Impact on the Lee County Dock Building Industry

There is no doubt that the dock building industry experienced negative economic impact from this action. Throughout an extended time period, dock builders have lived in uncertainty.

To obtain a better understanding of the situation, the graduate management strategy class of International College in Naples, Florida, conducted a survey of marine related businesses in Southwest Florida using a membership list provided by the FMCA. The purpose of this survey was to determine the extent of financial damage to the marine industry. (It should be noted that the survey was sent after the USFWS announced the lifting of the dock moratorium.)

FMCA members build, maintain, and repair residential and marina dock facilities throughout Florida. Family and commercial boaters use these facilities for recreation, business and employment. FMCA members also serve public welfare by dredging and maintaining waterway rights-of-way and by assisting in the building and maintenance of bridges, causeways, channels, canals, seawalls, and other marine structures vital to Florida's environment and its transportation and economic network.

The survey was mailed to 100 companies along with an explanation of International College's study on the dock moratorium's effect on business. Twelve surveys were returned indicating a response rate of 12%. FWC's projections estimated between 18-24 jobs would be lost; respondents to the survey reported 11.5. The average hourly wage for laid off workers was reported at $13.60.

Businesses responding to the survey also indicated a net reduction in gross revenues of 23%. Based on a review of expanded first time use codes, there are 26 dock builders in Lee County; their reported annual revenues range from under $500,000 to over $10,000,000. If the group's annual revenues are computed at the median range for the income levels indicated, the gross annual revenues for the 26 companies is $ 138,750,000. A 23% reduction of revenues translates to nearly $32,000,000.

With 14,409 homes on canals and 20,205 vacant waterfront lots in Cape Coral, it is easy to understand that dock building is big business. Most people want to protect expensive boats from the elements. Consequently, Cape Coral issued 1,272 permits in 2002 and 1,272 in 2003.

Keep in mind that the City of Cape Coral ignored the dock moratorium for most of the affected time. Cape Coral issued permits (see Table 7), then, relied on the contractor or homeowner to obtain federal permits. Essentially, they operated under a *don't ask, don't tell* system. Otherwise, the impact on dock builders would have been far greater. With the exception of the three-month period when USFWS issued a cease and desist order, builders in Cape Coral were able to operate.

Table 7. Cape Coral dock and boat lift permits.

	1999	2000	2001	2002	2003
Docks	1,255	1,511	1,866	2,331	2,338
Boat Lifts	707	884	940	1,272	1,234

Note. From Cape Coral Department of Community Development, (C. Schwing, personal communication, May 10, 2004).

However, this uncertainty itself caused many problems in the industry. Dock building companies reported anxiety among workers and many homeowners were confused by the constantly changing rules. As Figure 12 indicates, the economic value of the industry is significant with $12,195,000 worth of docks built in Cape Coral in 2002 and a record pace of $7,144,000 in the first six months of 2003.

Figure 12. Total permitting in yearly dollars.

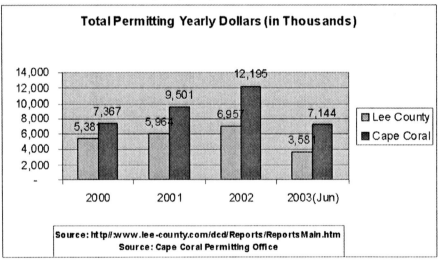

From Cape Coral Permitting Office. Retrieved May 5, 2003 from http://lee-county.com/dcd/reports/reportsmain.htm

The International College survey question, "Did your organization develop a strategic plan that would have enabled you to continue in business if you were to experience a loss in revenues?" yielded a 58% positive response. There were no details offered to clarify what type of plans were in place, but the dock moratorium had been an issue in Southwest Florida for over a year prior to the survey, and many dock builders were cautious as to the final outcome. One can presume that owners had plenty of incentive to plan strategically.

A report issued by USFWS predicted that Southwest Florida would experience substantial losses as described below (United States Fish and Wildlife Service, n.d.b).

- Year one: a decrease of $2.3 to $7.8 million, with a loss of 28 to 121 jobs
- Year two: a decrease of $3.1 to $14.0 million, with a loss of 41 to 227 jobs
- Year three: a decrease of $3.8 to $20.3 million, with a loss of 53 to 334 jobs
- Year four: a decrease of $0.5 to $20.3 million, with a loss of 66 to 440 jobs
- Year five: a decrease of $5.3 to $32.8 million, with a loss of 79 to 546 jobs

This report considered a continuing impact on yearly expenditures, with additional losses of marine access points, and continued flattening to declining demands for marine construction services. The report also addressed potential secondary effects on related sectors of the Florida economy such as employment.

> We also use IMPLAN to calculate the change in net employment. This analysis shows that there would be a loss of approximately 18 jobs from the direct, indirect and induced effects of limiting marine construction due to permitting restrictions continuing in the study area under baseline conditions (IMPLAN, n.d.).

Impact on Cape Coral Real Estate

Throughout this case study, much has been said about the impact on the real estate market in Cape Coral. The argument about economic impact of decisions concerning docks centers around statistics on sales of waterfront property. As noted in the City of Cape Coral's legal action and at public hearings, the prevailing feeling is that real estate sales have suffered due to restrictions placed on the building of docks. However, this issue remains muddy when you view statistics concerning the issue. The truth is that the manatee issue has caused an impact, but due to other economic factors driving sales, it will take a long-term study to determine the real impact of this issue.

To be fair to those analyzing this case, it is important to note that Cape Coral, founded over 40 years ago, is described as the largest and most successful master-planned community in the country. Prior to incorporation in 1970, city designers carefully planned the location of streets, canals, parks, public areas, transportation routes, commercial zones, and industrial parks. The emphasis was always on assuring that commercial and residential growth remained orderly, controlled, and balanced. Cape Coral has grown dramatically since its incorporation. In 1960 there was virtually no population. The city's metropolitan market area grew seven times faster than the national average in the 1980s. By 1995, the population had risen to approximately 85,000. Today, it is the most populous Florida gulf coast city south of Tampa. With approximately 40,000 of 135,000 building parcels occupied, the city has tremendous room for future growth.

The trend of investors buying property for immediate resale is slowing as property prices are increasing. The $200,000 lots on the market today that sold for $40,000 in 1999 have caused investors to look elsewhere while people who plan to occupy the land still consider the Cape a good deal when compared to Naples and Ft. Myers (Cull, 2004d).

Figure 13. Cape Coral saltwater homesites.

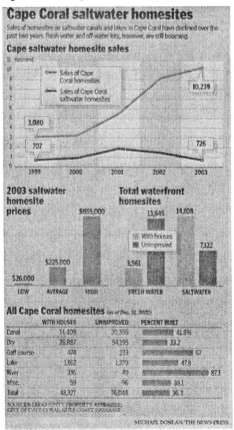

Due to the beauty of Cape Coral and over 400 miles of affordable waterfront property, the city has always been a target for land speculators. Between 2000 to 2001, prices of property took a dramatic change upward resulting in speculators turning to north Cape Coral and off water homes by 2004. In 2001, approximately 1,800 waterfront properties were sold. That number is reduced to 80 during the six month period from September 2003 to February 2004. The slowdown is blamed on one of two issues. Some believe that property prices have exceeded the real value while others are sure that uncertainty surrounding the dock building issue is slowing sales. Whatever the reason, buyers were at least temporarily looking elsewhere.

With 13,645 freshwater lots and 54,195 off water lots available, buyers can get a great deal. Freshwater lots sell for as low as $25,000 while saltwater lots may go for around $250,000 or more (see Figure 13).

From Cull, (2004d). Adapted with permission.

As noted in Table 8, building permits have not decreased over the past five years. Affordable property in Cape Coral continues to keep the building industry busy and new citizens moving to Cape Coral. So the question remains: is the glass half full or half empty in regards to the manatee/dock building issue? The area is booming but at a slower pace than in 2000 and 2001. Is the dock building permit issue the culprit or could inflated lot and home prices play a role?

To further illustrate this point, Table 9 shows samples of Cape Coral waterfront vacant lots over the past few years. Property value increases are an indication of growth in the real estate market in Cape Coral. As noted throughout this case, property values and home sales have increased at record rates over the past three years with no immediate end in sight.

Table 8. Single-family (SF), multi-family, and commercial permits–Cape Coral, Florida.

YEAR (SF)	Water (SF)	Non-water	Multi-Family	Commercial
1999	577	985	95	107
2000	632	993	69	96
2001	853	1,299	183	101
2002	799	1,848	216	198
2003	795	3,046	286	211

Note. From Cape Coral Department of Community Development, (C. Schwing, personal communication, May 10, 2004).

Table 9. Vacant waterfront lots.

Address	Purchase Date	Purchase Price	List Date	List Price	Percent %
2609 25th Ter SW	1/1/94	$100	11/25/04	$180,000	180,000%
2572 28th PL SW	4/1/79	$7,500	6/20/03	$229,000	3,053%
2548 26th PL SW	7/1/83	$8,700	3/21/04	$184,900	2,125%
2544 26th PL SW	9/1/83	$8,700	3/21/04	$184,900	2,125%
1925 34th Ter NE	8/3/99	$10,000	2/10/04	$53,000	530%
2623 29th Ave SW	5/1/97	$10,500	5/18/04	$205,000	1,952%
1717 33rd Ter NE	9/1/95	$17,000	1/28/04	$78,000	459%
3913 44th Ter NE	9/1/96	$18,500	3/18/04	$50,000	270%
2643 29th Ave SW	5/5/01	$19,500	4/13/04	$210,000	1,077%
2653 29th Ave SW	4/1/94	$27,000	4/7/04	$195,000	722%

2524 26th PL SW	8/1/00	$30,000	3/11/04	$169,000	566%
2834 30th St SW	3/1/97	$32,500	4/3/04	$170,000	523%
2516 25th St SW	4/20/03	$35,900	4/24/04	$227,900	635%
2733 28th Ave SW	7/1/01	$37,500	5/5/04	$225,000	600%
1623 38th PL NW	9/15/01	$40,000	3/29/04	$124,900	312%
3111 29th Ave SW	8/1/90	$44,000	3/13/04	$174,000	395%
2930 30th St SW	5/1/01	$46,000	4/13/04	$195,000	424%
2527 25th Ter SW	4/1/01	$47,500	5/5/04	$225,000	474%
2536 25th St SW	4/30/03	$48,000	3/5/04	$170,000	354%
2578 27th PL SW	4/30/03	$49,900	3/25/04	$239,000	479%
2810 30th St SW	4/30/03	$51,900	4/13/04	$195,000	376%
Surfside Blvd	3/3/01	$78,100	4/14/04	$325,000	416%
4912 1st Ct SW	4/1/90	$86,500	6/25/03	$315,000	364%
2856 26th PL SW	4/1/02	$89,900	4/22/04	$225,000	250%
3028 26th Ct SW	6/1/02	$109,900	5/8/04	$168,000	153%
2651 28th Ter SW	8/19/03	$113,000	5/11/04	$175,000	155%
2636 19th PL SE	9/28/01	$149,900	8/11/04	$259,900	173%
2700 25th St SW	4/1/02	$159,900	4/22/04	$349,000	218%
2709 28th Ave SW	10/16/02	$182,000	4/24/04	$272,900	150%
3124 Surfside Blvd	5/1/03	$251,000	2/2/04	$379,900	151%
1947 32nd Ter SW	2/13/04	$440,000	2/13/04	$699,900	159%

Note. Cape Coral Board of Realtors Multiple Listing. (n.d.). Retrieved June, 2004 from http://www.tropical-connections.com/nav.aspx/page=%2fpagemanager%2fdefault.aspx%2fpageid%3d391359

STATUS UPDATE: EVERY ACTION CAUSES AN EQUAL OR GREATER REACTION

As noted earlier, in November 2002, 10 Lee County boaters won their lawsuits against the State of Florida for speeding tickets on the basis that the placement of the manatee speed zones were not based on sound science and were unconstitutional. On January 28, 2004, the State of Florida's motion to appeal the ruling was denied (Call, 2004a). This was a victory for area boaters and a setback for local environmental groups. However, dock builders and homeowners proved to be caught in the middle.

A press release by USFWS on February 6, 2004, announced that in the wake of recent court rulings eliminating the manatee protection speed zones, the agency could no longer provide favorable reviews for new watercraft facilities requested by USACE. This includes permits for dock building within the zones designated as Estero Bay, Matlacha Pass, waterways near York and Galt Islands, the mouth of the Caloosahatchee River, near Shell Creek, and Punta Rassa (Call, 2004b). As a federal agency, the USFWS office made this ruling to enforce the 1973 ESA.

Immediately thereafter, 53 dock permits were placed on hold with no definitive solution in sight for these or future requests. Citing a Fort Myers judge's ruling in favor of area boaters and the botched appeal by attorneys representing the FWC, USFWS decided that federal rules must be enforced until an alternative could be analyzed and implemented (Gillis, 2004b).

The effects were felt heavily in Cape Coral, primarily the southwest area of Cape Coral. The constant changing of affected areas is confusing to dock builders and other members of the construction industry. According to the Chamber of Commerce and the CCCIA, the ruling will affect more than just dock builders with many in the industry depending on the ability to build docks on new or existing home sites. Cape Coral Councilmember and local realtor, Ms. Gloria Tate, indicated that she personally lost a $200,000 waterfront lot sale due to the ruling. City officials feel the current ruling will negatively affect suppliers, contractors, hardware stores, and many others dealing daily with the biggest industry in Lee County, Florida (Fischer, 2004c).

Public reaction to this latest ruling was immediate and angry with developers, dock builders, and citizens planning to purchase land or build a dock all commenting on the decision. Some dock builders rely heavily on customers located in the banned areas. Local realtors feel that potential customers will be deterred by the controversy and uncertainty surrounding the issue. Landowners waiting for approval to build docks are now frustrated with their inability to protect their boats or use the water they paid to be near. However, USFWS feels that until speed zones are in effect, they must enforce new rules to protect the manatee.

In an effort to break the stalemate that is holding up approval of dock permits, Lee County Commissioners decided to study the prospect of implementing temporary county speed zones. The action was met with mixed reaction as some commissioners were lukewarm about overlaying speed zones that a judge deemed unconstitutional. The City of Cape Coral cannot support the process due to its pending legal action, but will not oppose the move. Local dock builders deemed the effort as positive as long as it will satisfy the state requirements to release permits. The SMC felt this was a positive move and any effort to protect the manatee would be appreciated. Understandably, local boaters are not excited about a new speed zone to substitute for the one they just invalidated. However, to solve the building issue, Lee County has every right to take action as the state does not have to approve county action in this area (Cull, 2004a).

On February 24, 2004, Lee County Commissioners directed its staff to form a committee of stakeholders such as realtors, builders, boaters, environmentalists, and other affected parties to study a solution to the current crisis (Fischer, 2004a). However, before the committee could take action, USFWS replaced the invalidated state speed zones with emergency federal zones. This paved the way for the release of dock building permits, but it angered boaters who felt the federal government was getting involved in a local issue (Cull, 2004b).

To combat the rulings by state and federal agencies to impose speed zones and stop building permits for docks, a coalition of interested parties was formed. The coalition includes boaters' rights groups, local businesses, and some citizens of the City of Cape Coral who will lobby the US President and Florida Governor for a solution. The group does support the Alert Campaign developed by the Chamber of Commerce two years ago to communicate with government leaders about local issues. The first action was an email campaign to raise the level of awareness about this critical issue. The group is supported by other interested parties such as Standing Watch and the Cape Coral Construction Industry Association (Fischer, 2004b).

On March 2, 2004, the Second District Court of Appeal in Lakeland, Florida, denied the request from the FWC's request to overturn the Ft. Myers judge's ruling that the five manatee zones are unconstitutional. Therefore, the speed zones, as expected, no longer exist under state law. However, as mentioned earlier,

USFWS already superceded the action by adopting federal zones. The federal zones are not affected by the appellate court's ruling (Call & Cull, 2004a).

USFWS anticipates that once the temporary speed zones are in place, they will move forward immediately with the creation of permanent zones. USFWS is required to make the decision to move forward on creation of permanent zones within the first 10 days of the 120 days of declaration of an emergency action. The move leaves boaters, advocates, and community activists feeling that USFWS does not care about public opinion. However, the agency has promised that public forums will be a major part of the process to enact the federal laws in the affected areas (Fischer, 2004d). Lee County is still moving forward with their plans to create local speed zones with the hope that final federal zones will not be necessary.

CONCLUSION: THIS IS NOT OVER YET

This issue is far from solved. The constant on-again, off-again issuance of dock permits keeps this issue in the public eye. However, for the purpose of this case study, there must be a cutoff point. As this case progresses, there will be many twists and turns for years to come.

The recent 20th Judicial Circuit Court ruling that invalidated several local speed zones may seem a victory to some but could actually be a defeat of the worst kind. It was surprising how those involved in the case were unable to see the possible negative effects of their actions. Case in point, read the following quote from local attorney John Mills, in the March 3, 2004 edition of the Ft. Myers News-Press:

> It would be foolish for the feds to try and adopt the same rules that were just proven unconstitutional. I would be shocked at the arrogance of (the US) Fish & Wildlife (Service) if they tried to shut down the waters. It's [*sic*] total overkill (Call & Cull, 2004).

The removal of the zones could have widespread negative effects for the citizens of Lee County. It would be foolish to assume the federal government could or would not adopt similar speed zones due to the Schoonover ruling, as the federal threshold for creation of manatee refuges and sanctuaries (speed zones) under the ESA is significantly lower than that held by the state under the Florida Manatee Sanctuary Act. The federal government has the ability to create manatee protection areas (speed zones) whenever "there is substantial evidence showing such establishment is necessary to prevent the taking of one or more manatees" (United States Fish and Wildlife Service, n.d.b).

Due to the differences between the Florida statutes and the federal rulemaking process, the creation of federal zones would not be affected by the ruling in Mr. Mills' case. What the Schoonover ruling does accomplish is to open the door for the federal government to create emergency rules, effectively removing local control from an even larger portion of Lee County waters. In accordance with 50 CFR 17.106, the federal government can establish manatee protection areas on an emergency basis when *takings* are deemed to be imminent. It is safe to assume that in the eyes of the USFWS, removal of state manatee speed zones would certainly qualify as creating imminent possibility for take of manatee in Lee County. Potential establishment of new federal speed zones in Lee County has nothing to do with arrogance but rather the abilities of the USFWS under the law.

Based on these facts and previous federal actions, federal creation of speed zones which mirror the state zones that are currently unenforceable due to this ruling is a very real possibility. The federal government has the legal description of the effected zones in hand. Do the citizens of Lee County want more federal speed zones in Lee County waters, or would they rather have state speed zones where local citizens have some say and control over what is designed?

It is possible that the larger impact of the loss of these speeds zones will come in the permitting arena. USFWS evaluates three criteria when preparing Biological Opinions for single-family dock permits: presence of speed zones, adequate signage of speed zones, and enforcement presence in speed zones. The Schoonover ruling effectively removes two legs of this premise. This newly created lack of enforceable speed zones across portions of the county will allow USFWS to designate large portions of Lee County as areas of inadequate protection. This will expand the dock permitting situation to a broader moratorium which many have all worked hard to remedy.

On June 24, 2004, Governor Jeb Bush signed Senate Bill 540 requiring the FWC to study the population of manatees in areas such as utility plants where warm water is discharged. This action is praised by members of the construction and boating industries. Members of both industries agreed that this will help identify specific causes of manatee deaths and consider the rights of everyone involved (Fischer, 2004f). It is widely felt that this will demonstrate that boaters do not kill nearly as many manatees as reports indicate.

Additionally, in April 2004, FWC required that Lee County form a Local Rule Committee to review manatee speed zones in the county. This committee is comprised of two members appointed by each county commissioner and reports to FWC in August 2004. Each commissioner appointed one boater and one environmentalist to the committee in an effort to be fair (Fischer, 2004e). The committee is meeting as this case is being written and will forward its recommendations by August 10, 2004.

Environmentalists are getting more and more frustrated by the perception that the odds are stacked against them in Lee County. The Local Rule Committee is working to make speed zones less restrictive or eliminated all together and on June 29, 2004, county commissioners passed the Lee County Manatee Protection Plan that environmentalists feel offers little protection. In an interview on June 29, 2004, Laura Combs of the SMC was quoted as saying, "Manatees have been sold out in Lee County." However, members of the construction industry feel this plan opens up multi-slip docks for construction and allows for development (Fischer, 2004f). As noted throughout this case, there are no winners in this issue. Hopefully, businesses, government, and society will come together to find a solution that everyone can live with—especially the manatee.

CASE QUESTIONS

1. How does this case affect business, government, and society stakeholders? Do they agree on the issues?

2. What were the government agencies trying to accomplish by their initial actions to protect the manatee in response to the settlement agreement with environmentalists? What were those actions?

3. This case study was cut off in July of 2004. However, it is an ongoing issue in Southwest Florida. What actions have occurred since this case study ended? What sources did you use to determine your answer?

4. What was the economic impact on the dock building industry? Justify your response.

5. What was the overall economic impact on Cape Coral Florida? Were real estate values affected? Justify your response.

6. What was the local government's role in this issue? Were the policies initiated effective? What policies could have been initiated?

7. Update the legal action filed by the City of Cape Coral via Internet research. Was this legal action necessary? Was it effective?

8. What role did USFWS play in this controversial issue? Were they effective? What strategic initiatives would you suggest to satisfy the concerns of all parties while still protecting the manatee?

9. Examine the role of environmental groups. Were their actions effective? Did they receive the desired outcomes?

10. What future strategies would you suggest?

PRACTICAL EXERCISE OR GROUP PROJECT

Using information from this case study and updated research, prepare an analysis and recommendations to be presented in class. Think of yourselves as consultants who are working for any of the agencies involved the case. Your assignment is to analyze their process, financial documentation, and prepare a report to present to the Governor of Florida.

In your report, you should outline an *Action Plan* stating what must be done and why. The questions about the case are merely guidelines to think through. Do not make your case report a question/answer document. Think of the course material that you have studied and select applicable issues and models.

A good case report starts with a one page *Executive Summary*, geared to the busy executive who may not have time to read all of the report. In the Executive Summary, state clearly what your recommendations are and why; do not go into detail; leave that for the main body of the report.

The report should not exceed three pages with the exception of calculations or figures that may be attached in an appendix. The report must be typed, but calculations or figures could be hand written neatly. In the report, you should go into more detail about your recommendations and justify them using the facts about the case. Support your conclusions and recommendations.

REFERENCES

About FWC. (2004, July). Florida Fish and Wildlife Conservation Commission, retrieved October 15, 2004 from http://myfwc.com/aboutus/aboutfwc.html

Boat registrations hit record high. (2004, May 6). *Cape Coral Daily Breeze*, pp. A1, A8.

Call, C. L. (2004a, January 29). Five manatee zones can't be enforced. *The News-Press*, pp. A1, A3.

Call, C. L. (2004b, February 11). Dock permits halted. *The News-Press*, retrieved from http://www.news-press.com/news/local_state/040210manatees.html

Call, C. L. & Cull, J. (2004, March 3). Five state manatee zones erased. *The News-Press*, pp. A1, B1.

Cape Coral Board of Realtors Multiple Listing. (n.d.). Retrieved May 2004 from http://www.tropical-connections.com/nav.aspx/page=%2fpagemanager%2fdefault.aspx%2fpageid%3d391359

Cape Coral Construction Industry Association. (n.d.). Retrieved December 29, 2003, from http://www.cccia.org

Cape Coral Permitting Office. Retrieved May 5, 2003 from http://lee county.com/dcd/reportsmain.htm

Cull, J. (2002, December 13). Boat dock laws to be examined. *The News Press, The Cape*, pp. A1, B1.

Cull, J. (2003a, January 14). Speed zones may get tighter. *The News Press*. Retrieved from http://news-press.com/news/environment/p_030114manatee.html

Cull, J. (2003b, January 16). Manatee count down locally, but up in state. *The News-Press*, retrieved from http://news-press.com/news/environment/p_030116manateecount.html.

Cull, J. (2003c, May 5). Controversy in rule's wake–Dock builders, contractors, homeowners and officials say the new manatee rule will hurt the local economy. *The News-Press, pp.* 1A, 10A.

Cull, J. (2003d, October 24). Manatee club's mission, supporters have changed. *The News Press*, retrieved from http://news-press.com/news/environment/030505manateeclub.html

Cull, J. (2004a, February 20). Lee seeks manatee solution. *The News-Press*, retrieved from http://www.news-press.com/news/local_state/040220manatees.html

Cull, J. (2004b, February 27). Lee waterway speed zones back in play. *The News-Press*, retrieved from http://www.news-press.com/news/local_state/040227manatee.html

Cull, J. (2004c, February 29). Freshwater properties hot item. *The News Press*, pp. A1, A2.

Cull, J. (2004d, April 7). Canal-front property becomes the hot spot–prices soar as area has grown. *The News-Press, pp.* A1, A3.

Cull, J. (2004e, June 3). City's legal fees beginning to add up–Cape bill $400,000 for outside law firms. *The News Press, The Cape,* pp. A1, A5.

Cull, J. & Hayford, P. (2003, May 14). Zone foes dominate hearing–Volatile boating speed proposal draws 2,500. *The News Press*, retrieved from http://wwwnews-press.com/news/environment/p_030514manateehearing.html

Duffy, K. (2003a, May 7). Save The Manatee Club calls rules withdrawal positive. *Cape Coral Daily Breeze*, pp. 1A, 9A.

Duffy, K. (2003b, May 14). Feds lift "Area of Inadequate Protection" designation. *Cape Coral Daily Breeze*, pp. 1A, 6A.

Endangered Outlaw. (n.d.). Retrieved May 5, 2003, from www.endangeredoutlaw.com/designs.htm

ESA. (n.d.) The Endangered Species Act of 1973. Retrieved October 27, 2004 from http://endangered.fws.gov/esa.html

Fischer, D. (2004a, February 25). County to form waterway speed-zone committee. *Cape Coral Daily Breeze*, pp. 1A, 2A.

Fischer, D. (2004b, March 2). Council urges approval of county manatee protection plan. *Cape Coral Daily Breeze*, pp. 1A, 3A.

Fischer, D. (2004c, March 3). Coalition to direct speed zone concerns to president, governor. *Cape Coral Daily Breeze*, pp. 1A, 3A.

Fischer, D. (2004d, March 4). U.S. Fish moves to make speed zones permanent. *Cape Coral Daily Breeze*, pp. 1A, 3A.

Fischer, D. (2004e, June 24). Locals react to Bush's OK of manatee study mandate. *Cape Coral Daily Breeze*, pp. A1, A3.

Fischer, D. (2004f, June 30). Manatee plan approved 5-0: Save the Manatee Club unhappy. *Cape Coral Daily Breeze*, pp. A1, A2.

Florida Fish and Wildlife Conservation Commission. (n.d.a). Retrieved May 5, 2002, from http://myfwc.com/manatee/rules.htm

Florida Fish and Wildlife Conservation Commission. (n.d.b). Retrieved September 16, 2004, from http//northflorida.fws.gov/manatee/maps/lee-overview.htm

Florida Fish and Wildlife Conservation Commission Manatee Mortality Database. Retrieved May 5, 2003, from http://www.floridamarine.org/manatees/search_summary.asp

Florida Marine Contractors Association. (n.d.). Retrieved May 5, 2003, from http://www.flmarinecontractors.org

Florida Marine Industry. (n.d.). Retrieved December 29, 2003, from http://www.boatflorida.org

Florida Marine Research Institute, Yearly Mortality Summaries. (n.d.). Retrieved May 5, 2003, from http://research.myfwc.com/manatees/search_summary.asp

FWC. (n.d.). Retrieved May 5, 2002 from http://myfwc.com/manatee/rules.htm

Gillis, C. (2003a, February 26). Lee manatee protection plan called 'woefully constructed'. *Naples Daily News*, p. A1.

Gillis, C. (2003b, March 27). State puts gag order on manatee experts. *Naples Daily News*, pp. A1, A4.

Gillis, C. (2003c, November 17). State considers dropping manatee off endangered list. *Naples Daily News*. Retrieved from http://www1.naplesnews.com/npdn/news/article/0,2071,NPDN_14940_2433884,00.html

Gillis, C. (2004, February 11). Agency ruling puts 53 dock permits on hold. *Naples Daily News*, retrieved from http://www.naplesnews.com/npdn/bonitanews/article/0,2071,NPDN_14894_2645105,00

Lee County Economic Development Council. (n.d.a). Retrieved May 5, 2003, from http://www.leecountybusiness.com

Lee County Economic Development Council. (n.d.b). Retrieved May 5, 2003, from http://www.leecountybusiness.com/communityoverview/population/population.html

Marine Mammal Protection Act. (n.d.). DOE environmental policy and guidance Retrieved October 15, 2004, from http://www.eh.doe.gov/oepa/laws/mmpa.html

Save the Manatee Club. (n.d.). Retrieved December 28, 2003 from http://www.savethemanatee.org

Service looking to develop special regulations for Florida Manatees under the Marine Mammal Protection Act. (2001, March 13). U.S. Fish & Wildlife Service, retrieved September 9, 2004 from http://northflorida.fws.gov/releases-01/003-01-mmpa-regs.htm

Standing Watch. (n.d.). Retrieved December 29, 2003, from http://www.standing-watch.org

The Endangered Species Act of 1973. (n.d.). U.S. Fish & Wildlife Service. Retrieved September 14, 2004, from http://endangered.fws.gov/esa.html#Lnk02

United States Army Corps of Engineers. (n.d.). Retrieved December 28, 2003, from http://www.usace.army.mil/

United States Census Bureau. (n.d.). Retrieved May 5, 2004, from http://quickfacts.census.gov/qfd/maps/florida_map.html

United States Fish and Wildlife Conservation Commission. (n.d.a). Retrieved August 5, 2004a, from http://training.fws.gov/library/pubs/conserving.pdf

United States Fish and Wildlife Conservation Commission. (n.d.b). Retrieved September 20, 2004b, from http://myfwc.com/

United States Fish and Wildlife Service. (n.d.a). Retrieved May 4, 2003 from http://www.fws.gov/

United States Fish and Wildlife Service. (n.d.b). Retrieved May 5, 2003, from http://northflorida.fws.gov/Manatee/Maps/lee-overview.htm

Whitehead, C. (2002, December 14). Gov. Bush: Dock moratorium for manatees a disaster. *Naples Daily News*, p. A1

Yearly Mortality Summaries. (2004). Florida Marine Research Institute–Florida fish and Wildlife Conservation Commission. Retrieved May 5, 2003 from http://www.floridamarine.org/features/view_article.asp?id=12084.htm

APPENDIX A—THE ACADEMIC EVENT

Overview of the Round Table Discussion (August 12, 2003)
Manatee vs. Economics:
The Cape Coral Florida Experience
An Integrated Case Study

Three International College Professors, Dr. Kris Thoemke, Dr. Telemate Jackreece, and Dr. Don Forrer, integrated Summer 2003 International College graduate courses through group projects to study the ongoing manatee/dock building issue in Southwest Florida from an academic perspective. The main purpose was to integrate this important issue in an academic setting where several graduate classes from the School of Business analyzed the independent viewpoints from three sectors: environment, government, and business. The result of this project was an open forum, round table discussion on Tuesday, August 12, 2003, at the Cape Coral Yacht Club. Cape Coral was selected because it is the center of this controversial issue.

The forum included Dr. Thoemke's class (Environmental Permitting and Compliance) which evaluated the environmental concerns, then analyzed the federal and state regulations that brought this issue to the forefront. Dr. Jackreece's classes (Public Administration, Function and Structure & Public Policy Analysis) examined the public viewpoint centering on procedures for implementation of the regulations that resulted from the SMC legal action. Dr. Forrer's classes (Strategic Business Management & Management Processes) analyzed the business impact. Each professor provided guidance as his class prepared for the presentation and discussion.

The round table began with each student group presenting an academic analysis of this issue through four perspectives: 1) Environmental, 2) Regulatory, 3) Public Administration, and 4) Business. Then followed a discussion among leaders from each affected area and the five International College classes involved to clarify research questions. At the end of the session, input was allowed from members of the public.

Invited panelists included key leaders from all affected areas. The event was moderated by Jessica Stilwell of NBC2 News and was attended by over 150 citizens. Rotary Club of Cape Coral sponsored the event as a public service.

The experience and knowledge gained by International College graduate students proved invaluable. What began as a method of verifying research turned out to be a unique educational experience. The setting was that of a town hall meeting with most of the 150 members of the audience supporting the dock building industry and hostile to the views of environmentalists. Normally, International College students present their work and receive praise from their fellow classmates and a grade from the professor. However, this forum produced cheers for data supporting the industry position and jeers for anything supporting the enviromental view. This atmosphere provided an awesome setting for an academic event.

The ability to replicate a civic meeting where the audience is partial to oneside was deemed a coup by event organizers. Students usually only get to witness this type of meeting. Our students were active participants and usually under fire from the audience. Additionally, while more professional, the panel was very quick to challenge research conducted by students when it did not support their public position. A DVD copy of the event may be obtained by contacting the bookstore at International College.

The following biographical material was furnished by each of the featured panelists.

Ms. Jessica Stilwell—Moderator

Jessica Stilwell is the co-anchor for NBC2 News in Ft. Myers, Florida. Jessica has been employed by Waterman Broadcasting since March of 1997. Before coming here, she was a reporter/anchor for a cable station in Naples, WB10. She graduated from the University of Southern California in 1995 with a B.A. in Journalism and Political Science.

Mr. Terry Stewart—Cape Coral City Manager

Mr. Stewart was born in Wilmington, North Carolina and has been a resident of Florida since 1964. He is married with two children and holds a B.S. in Business Administration from Nova University plus a Masters in Public Administration from Nova Southeastern University. Terry's experience includes Assistant City Manager of Pembroke Pines, Assistant Fire Chief for the city of Pembroke Pines, Fire Chief for the city of Lauderdale Lakes, United Way Campaign Manager for nine years, Chamber of Commerce Board of Director 1997 thru 1998, Chamber Pinnacle Award 1998, Arts & Culture Advisory Board Liaison, Adjunct Professor of Nova Southeastern University and Broward Community College, and High School Student Mentor for Broward School Enterprise Ambassador's program. Terry's personal interests include theater, singing, motorcycles, fishing, and handcraft hobbies.

Ms. Alexandria LePera—District 5 Cape Coral Council

Ms. LePera is a former educator with degrees in Health, Physical Education and Recreation as well as English. She moved to Cape Coral in 1988 from Pittsburgh, PA, where she was an office manager for a hospital/emergency medical services supply corporation. She has been politically involved since the days of JFK. Since living in Cape Coral, she has served on a multitude of boards and associations including the Community Re-development Agency, the Community Development Block Grant Advisory Board, and has been a proud member of the Lee County Land Acquisition & Stewardship Advisory Committee (Conservation 20/20) since 1998. She has been married for fifteen (15) years and is involved in several community activities such as the Southwest Florida Symphony Society, Code Enforcement Task Force (vice-chair), Cape Coral Police Department (volunteer), and Legislature Review board (chairperson).

Mr. Andy Coy—Lee County Commissioner District 4

A passion for education led Andy Coy to a 12-year career in the Lee County Public School System. A passion for service ultimately led him to a seat on the Lee County Board of County Commissioners. Andy began his 26 years as a Lee County resident when he attended North Fort Myers High School. He went on to Edison Community College and received his BA and MA degrees from the University of Florida and University of South Florida, respectively. Andy lives in Cape Coral with his wife, Lisa, and daughters Aubrey and Chelsey. He and his family are members of the McGregor Baptist Church. He remains involved in the education community by serving on the Partners in Education Council, Golden Apple Scholarship Committee, and Take Stock in Children Leadership Council. He considers it a joy and a blessing to be a public servant for the people of Lee County.

Mr. Ron Carlock—Cape Coral Rotary President

Mr. Carlock is currently the President of the Cape Coral Rotary Club and of Carlock & Associates Insurance. He is also a member of the Cape Coral Chamber of Commerce and the Cape Coral Council for Progress. Mr. Carlock has a BA and an MBA from the University of Kansas. Also, Mr. Carlock was a past President of the Lee County Independent Insurance Agents.

Mr. John Kinney—Vice President of Standing Watch

John Kinney is a retired Fire Line Officer from the Washington, D.C. Fire Department, who moved to Cape Coral with his wife in 1991 to enjoy the weather and fishing. He joined the Cape Coral Tarpon Hunters Club in 1992 and has been on their Board of Directors for the past 11 years. In 1996 he was asked to write the club's position on proposed speed zones on the Caloosahatchee River that Lee County was proposing. He also contributed a response to FWC and the USFWS to aid in their proposed rule making process. In 2001 he heard about an organization called Standing Watch, a newly formed group that was developed to fight for boater's rights to use Florida's waterways. It was shortly after he joined that he started a Lee County Chapter and became the director.

Ms. Margaret Emblidge—Director of Planning for Bonita Bay Group

As Director of Planning, Ms. Emblidge is responsible for the coordination of the master planning and permitting for all projects developed by The Bonita Bay Group and for coordinating legislative initiatives on the federal, state, and local level. Ms. Emblidge has 17 years of experience in real estate development and land use planning including developments of regional impact, comprehensive planning, zoning approvals, and land development regulations. She has worked extensively with legislative, regulatory, and permitting agencies, along with special interest groups on creating public policy improvements. Prior to joining The Bonita Bay Group in 1996, Ms. Emblidge worked for more than five years as a planner for the Lee County Department of Community Development. Before moving to Florida, Ms. Emblidge worked for the Delaware County Planning Department in Media, PA, and prior to that as a real estate agent. Ms Emblidge was appointed by Governor Jeb Bush to the Southwest Florida Regional Planning Council and is a member of the Bonita Springs Chamber of Commerce Government Affairs Committee, the American Institute of Certified Planners, the American Planning Association, the Florida Planning and Zoning Association, and the Urban Land Institute. She holds a bachelor's degree in Geography and a master's degree in Urban and Regional Planning.

Mr. Kenneth Stead—Executive Director Southwest Florida Marine Industries Association

A graduate of Ohio University, Ken has served as the Executive Director of the Southwest Florida Marine Industries Association for the past seven years. He currently serves on the Board of Directors of the Marine Industries Association of

Florida and is a member of the Clean Boating Partnership as well as holding the designation of Certified Marina Manager. A lifelong boater, he has been a live aboard sailor, an offshore powerboat racer, and boated extensively on the Great Lakes, Florida and the Caribbean. Ken has been involved at the local, state and federal level with manatee protection issues for over 15 years. He currently directs the attorneys for the interveners in the most recent lawsuit filed by the Save the Manatee Club and has represented industry at numerous workshops and forums. He advocates a balanced science-based approach to manatee protection.

Ms. Laura Combs—Save the Manatee Club

Laura Ruhana Combs began her work on manatee protection in January 1991 with the state of Florida's Bureau of Protected Species Management (BPSM), which now resides in the FWC. In 1991, Laura also earned her Master's degree in Urban and Regional Planning, with a specialty in environmental planning, from Florida State University. While with the BPSM for seven years, she worked with local, state and federal governments, citizens, businesses and other private groups to develop manatee protection speed zones and manatee protection plans, among many other duties. Laura currently heads the Save the Manatee Club's southwest regional office and focuses her efforts on manatee protection issues in Charlotte, Lee and Collier counties.

Mr. Michael McCartney—Owner of American Marine Construction of Southwest Florida

Raised in Alaska before moving to Florida in 1989, Mr. McCartney has been building docks for 13 years and has been a licensed marine contractor for 9 years. He has operated American Marine Construction of South Florida, Inc. based in Cape Coral, FL, since 1994 and is a member of the Cape Coral Construction Association and the Florida Marine Contractors Association where he sits on the Licensing and Building Standards Committee and chairs the Future Association Goals Committee. Mr. McCartney is an Assistant Director of the Lee County Chapter of Standing Watch, a boater's coalition, and is a member of the Cape Coral Coalition and the Lee County Water Access Coalition. He has been very active on the issues relating to the manatee and government regulation during the past three years.

Ms. Patti Schnell—Executive Director—Cape Coral Construction Industry Association

Patti Schnell is a native Floridian and attended college at the University of Florida where she received her Bachelor of Science degree in Broadcast Journalism. Patti's career has been primarily in working with non-profit organizations. She was Assistant Director of the Key West Chamber of Commerce, worked as Special Events Coordinator for the Cape Coral Chamber of Commerce, served as the Executive Director of the North Fort Myers Chamber of Commerce, and is now the Executive Director of the CCCIA, where she has served for over five years. In addition to Patti's responsibilities with the CCCIA, she also serves on the Steering Committee of Red White & BOOM, and is on the Board of Directors of the Octagon Animal Showcase. She is also a proud member of the Cape Coral Gold Coast Rotary Club.

AUTHORS' NOTE

The research for this case study was conducted from May 2003 through July 2004. A roundtable discussion was conducted on August 12, 2003. The case transcends boundary lines for numerous disciplines of study. This project involved International College students primarily from three fields of study: business administration, environmental management, and public administration, but could have easily included a number of other disciplines. The beauty of this case is that it is far from concluded and can be studied for many years to come. The political aspects of business and influence of civic groups cannot be ignored as this case is analyzed.

It is the authors' intention to present this case as it is viewed by various stakeholders and the community as a whole. The case attempts to capture the action/reaction of business, government, and society as the situation evolved. This case is not inclusive of every aspect or action taken during this time period. There is plenty of material for future researchers to ponder as the case is reevaluated. Pending and future legal action will most certainly cause reaction from the affected parties.

LIST OF FIGURES

LIST OF ACRONYMS

CCCIA	Cape Coral Construction Industry Association
ESA	Endangered Species Act
DCA	Florida Department of Community Affairs
FDEP	Florida Department of Environmental Protection
FMCA	Florida Marine Contractors Association
FMI	Florida Marine Industry
MBA	Master of Business Administration
MEM	Master of Environmental Management
MMPA	Marine Mammal Protection Act
MPA	Master of Public Administration
MPP	Manatee Protection Plan
USACE	United States Army Corps of Engineers
USFWS	United States Fish and Wildlife Service
FWC	Florida Fish and Wildlife Conservation Commission
BPSM	Bureau of Protected Species Management

0-595-33784-8

Printed in the United States
25322LVS00005B/64-165

9 780595 337842